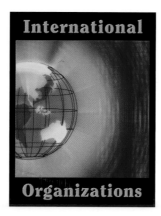

United Nations

Frank Tarsitano

WORLD ALMANAC® LIBRARY

Please visit our web site at: www.worldalmanaclibrary.com
For a free color catalog describing World Almanac® Library's list
of high-quality books and multimedia programs, call 1-800-848-2928 (USA)
or 1-800-387-3178 (Canada). World Almanac® Library's fax: (414) 332-3567.

Library of Congress Cataloging-in-Publication Data

Tarsitano, Frank.
    United Nations / by Frank Tarsitano.
       p. cm. — (International organizations)
    Includes bibliographical references and index.
    Contents: Searching for peace — Meeting place of the world — Taking on other tasks —
The peacekeepers — Agents of assistance.
    ISBN 0-8368-5523-X (lib. bdg.)
    ISBN 0-8368-5532-9 (softcover)
    1. United Nations—Juvenile literature. [1. United Nations.] I. Title. II. International
organizations (Milwaukee, Wis.)
    JZ4984.6.T37 2003
    341.23—dc21   2003045034

First published in 2004 by
World Almanac® Library
330 West Olive Street, Suite 100
Milwaukee, WI 53212 USA

Developed by Books Two, Inc.
Editor: Jean B. Black
Design and Maps: Krueger Graphics, Inc.: Karla J. Krueger and Victoria L. Buck
Indexer: Chandelle Black
World Almanac® Library editor: JoAnn Early Macken
World Almanac® Library art direction: Tammy Gruenewald

Photo Credits: All photos courtesy United Nations Photo Library, except: © AP Photo/Jim Collins: 38;
© APF/CORBIS: 32; Audiovisual Library European Commission: 28; Library of Congress: 7, 22;
© Marcel Crozet/WHO: 26

Printed in the United States of America

1 2 3 4 5 6 7 8 9 07 06 05 04 03

TABLE OF CONTENTS

Words that appear in the glossary are printed in
boldface type the first time they occur in the text.

Chapter One

Searching for Peace

Timor is an island at the eastern end of the 2,500-mile chain of islands making up Indonesia. Timor was divided between the Portuguese and the Dutch more than three hundred years ago. Each half developed very differently. East Timor, separated from the Dutch-held west by high mountains, was Portuguese. When Portugal withdrew in 1974, Indonesia sent in troops and declared East Timor a province. The people of East Timor fought against the Indonesian action, and several hundred thousand died from the war and famine in the following years.

In 1982, the United Nations (UN) stepped in. The UN is an organization made up of almost all independent nations on Earth. An important part of the UN's work is to keep the peace when different nations conflict with each other. The UN had never recognized Indonesia's right to East Timor, so it held a long series of talks between the authorities of East Timor and Indonesia to resolve the conflict. Finally, in 1998, Indonesia's president proposed that East Timor could have its own government if it would accept being part of Indonesia. The UN agreed to oversee the voting process to see whether the East Timorese would agree. Violence grew as pro-Indonesian fighters from Indonesian West Timor attacked at random, hoping to frighten the East Timorese into not breaking away. Many pro-Indonesian East Timorese fled to safety in West Timor. Those people in the east who favored independence had nowhere to go.

The UN at Work

During the following years, many different branches of the United Nations played roles in turning East Timor into an independent nation. The General Assembly, which is the body made up of representatives of all member nations, approved the UN's oversight of the voting process. Some UN representatives sent to East Timor by the UN peacekeepers were attacked, and some were killed. In the weeks before the voting, rallies both for and against the proposal were held, and some of the people who favored independence were killed.

On August 30, 1999, the East Timorese people voted 78.5 percent to 21.5 percent against becoming part of the Republic of Indonesia. The violence worsened in the eastern part of the island. Additional thousands of East Timorese who had voted against independence took refuge in West Timor. The UN **refugee**-aid section, called the UN High Commission for Refugees, worked to feed and shelter the refugees in the West Timor camps.

The UN Security Council is the fifteen-member UN body with the main responsibility for keeping peace throughout the world. The Security Council authorized a multinational peacekeeping force, headed by Australia, to go into East Timor and calm the situation. The Security Council also established the UN Transitional Administration in East Timor to administer the territory and help East Timor develop self-government. After several mass graves were found, the UN Economic and Social Council sent experts from the UN Commission on Human Rights to look into **human rights** violations.

Despite the continuing violence, the East Timorese people gradually took over the tasks of running their own country. On August 30, 2001, they freely voted for members of their own legislative assembly in their first democratic election. They drew up the nation's first constitution, and on May 20, 2002, East Timor became the independent nation officially called Timor-Leste. The following September, it proudly became the 191st member of the United Nations, the organization that had used some of its many functions to help turn East Timor into a nation.

In a ceremony on United Nations Plaza in New York City, East Timor's new flag was raised in recognition of the country's admission to the UN.

A Short History

The goal of the United Nations is clearly stated in the Preamble, or introduction, to the UN **Charter**: "We, the peoples of the United Nations [are] determined to save succeeding generations from the scourge of war . . ." This preamble was written in 1945 just as World War II was ending. About fifty million people died in that war, and the nations that were winning the war wanted to create an organization that might prevent future wars from breaking out.

The United Nations can trace its roots back to the League of Nations, which was formed as part of the Versailles Peace Treaty signed in 1919, the year after World War I ended. The League of Nations had little real power of its own; it depended on member nations for support. Its headquarters was in Geneva, Switzerland.

Not all the countries that fought in World War I joined the League. The most important country to reject the League was the United States, even though it was U.S. President Woodrow Wilson who had proposed the idea of an international peacekeeping organization in the first place. Powerful forces in the United States opposed becoming involved in European affairs again, and these forces helped bring about rejection of the League by the U.S. Senate.

Without the United States, the League proved to be very weak. Aggressive nations took advantage of this weakness. In 1931, Japan invaded Manchuria (now part of China) and set up a **puppet government** there. When the League condemned Japan's action, Japan withdrew from the League. In 1933, Germany, too, withdrew. When Italy was condemned by the League for invading Ethiopia, Italy also left the League.

Failure after failure continued to doom the League, and when World War II began in Europe in 1939, the League had no power to stop it. Although the League remained alive on paper during that war, it was essentially a dead organization. It finally was officially dissolved in 1946. By that time, the nations of the world were creating a new international organization called the United Nations. This time, the United States joined.

World War II

World War II began in Europe in September 1939 when German troops invaded Poland, which had mutual-defense treaties with the United Kingdom and France. Both these countries declared war on Germany. By the end of 1940, Germany had conquered most of Western Europe, and in 1941, the Germans invaded the Soviet Union.

Woodrow Wilson (1856-1924)

Woodrow Wilson was an idealist who believed deeply in America and in democracy. He took office as the twenty-eighth president of the United States in 1913 and remained president until 1921.

Wilson believed in the right of all people to be free and to choose their own form of government. The League of Nations was one of Wilson's ideas for keeping peace after the horrors of World War I.

Wilson became very ill in 1919 while traveling throughout the United States trying to gain support for the League of Nations. He was too ill to continue his task of persuading the American people that the United States should join the international organization, and in 1920, the U.S. Senate voted against membership in the League. The League had little chance of long-term success without the United States.

Shapers of the UN

During World War II, the three most powerful men on the Allied side were Winston Churchill (left), Franklin Delano Roosevelt (right), and Joseph Stalin. Churchill and Roosevelt were the leaders of the two greatest democracies in the world, the United Kingdom and the United States. Stalin was the Communist dictator of the Soviet Union. The three countries had come together as allies only to defeat the common enemy of Nazi Germany.

Churchill, Roosevelt, and Stalin agreed that some kind of world organization would be needed to try to keep peace after World War II, but the "Big Three" could not agree on how the new organization should be set up. They met twice to work out the framework of the new organization and hash out the differences they had. Despite these differences, the "Big Three" reached a compromise on how the new organization should be structured.

Later, the differences between the democracies and the Communists developed into a conflict known as the "**Cold War.**" At times, it looked as if this political struggle might destroy the United Nations, but when the Soviet Union collapsed in 1989-90, the organization seemed to become stronger than ever.

The United States entered the war in December 1941 after Japan attacked the U.S. naval base at Pearl Harbor, Hawaii. The attack destroyed much of the U.S. Pacific fleet as it lay at anchor on a peaceful Sunday morning. The United States joined the United Kingdom, the Soviet Union, and China as one of the Allied Powers. France had already been conquered by the Germans, but the Free French in France's colonies and the French forces that had escaped to England fought on the Allied side during the war and were officially considered an Allied Power.

Opposing the Allies were the Axis Powers—Germany, Italy, Japan, and a few smaller European countries. When the war ended in 1945 with victory for the Allied Powers, the victorious nations created a new international organization dedicated to peace—the United Nations.

During World War II, Franklin Delano Roosevelt was president of the United States, Winston Churchill was prime minister of the United

Kingdom, and Joseph Stalin was premier of the Soviet Union. These men, known as the "Big Three," worked together to shape the outline of the new international organization they hoped would work for world peace. In August 1944, representatives of the Allied Powers met at Dumbarton Oaks, a mansion in Washington, D.C., to put together proposals for the development of the new United Nations. These proposals described the goals and structure of the organization.

Representatives of fifty nations met in San Francisco in April 1945, just as the war was ending in Europe, to discuss the Dumbarton Oaks Proposals. The job of the representatives was to draw up a charter for the United Nations. The charter is like a constitution because it lays out the basic rules, goals, and structure of the organization. All the nations at the conference had an equal vote in all discussions, and decisions were made by a two-thirds majority vote.

The UN Charter called for six major organs, or branches, of the UN. The General Assembly, the largest organ, is made up of representatives of all the member nations, and each member nation has an equal vote. There are also five other major organs:

• a Security Council, which has five permanent members—the United States, the United Kingdom, the Soviet Union (now Russia), France, and China—and members appointed by the General Assembly

On June 26, 1945, representatives of fifty nations signed the UN Charter (the book at the right), surrounded by the flags of all those nations. President Harry Truman signed for the United States.

9

- a General Assembly
- an Economic and Social Council to deal with social problems
- a Secretariat to handle the UN's paperwork
- a Trusteeship Council to supervise nonindependent lands
- an International Court of Justice to make decisions about international law

On June 25, 1945, the nations voted to approve the charter that had been worked out. No nation voted against the charter. The next day, the representatives of the fifty nations at the conference signed the charter and sent it to their governments to be ratified, or approved.

The U.S. Senate approved the United Nations Charter by a vote of 89 to 2. President Harry S. Truman signed the approval on August 8, 1945, as the United States officially became part of the UN.

October 24 is United Nations Day, commemorating the day in 1945 by which the founding nations had ratified the charter.

By October 24, 1945, the governments of a majority of the nations attending the San Francisco conference had approved the charter. The United Nations became a reality on that day, which is now known as United Nations Day.

The fledgling United Nations began its work in temporary quarters in London, England, in early 1946. The permanent headquarters was built in New York City. The employees moved there in 1952.

Membership

According to the UN Charter, membership in the United Nations is open to all nations that promise to support peace and agree to carry out the principles stated in the UN Charter. New member nations must be recommended by the Security Council and approved by the General Assembly.

One nation in particular, China, had a tough time getting into the United Nations.

We the peoples of the United 🌐 Nations

We the peoples

A 1940s poster showed the public that the Charter of the new United Nations started out with almost the same words as the Constitution of the United States.

The Preamble, or opening words, to the Charter of the United Nations:

"We the peoples of the United Nations determined to save succeeding generations from the scourge of war which twice in our lifetimes has brought untold sorrow to mankind,

and to reaffirm faith in fundamental human rights, in the dignity and worth of human beings, in the equal rights of men and women and of nations large and small,

and to establish conditions under which justice and the respect for the obligations arising from treaties and other sources of international law can be maintained,

and to promote social progress and better standards of life in larger freedom,

and for these ends to practice tolerance and live together in peace with one another as good neighbors,

and to unite our strength to maintain international peace and security,

and to ensure, by the acceptance of principles and the institution of methods, that armed force shall not be used, save in the common interest,

and to employ international machinery for the promotion of the economic and social advancement of all peoples, have resolved to combine our efforts to accomplish these aims.

Accordingly, our respective governments, through representatives assembled in the city of San Francisco . . . do hereby establish an international organization to be known as the United Nations."

The Republic of China was one of the five major Allied Powers that won World War II, and it was deeply involved in forming the United Nations. Before the war and soon after, however, China was split by a civil war with one side, the Communists, led by Mao Zedong, and the other side, the Nationalists, led by General Chiang Kai-shek.

In 1946, most of the world recognized the Nationalists as the official government of China, and representatives from Chiang Kai-shek's

Even today, China and Taiwan both claim to represent the Chinese people.

government helped create the UN Charter. Chiang's Nationalist government took China's seat in the UN. The Republic of China became a permanent member of the Security Council, and like all permanent members, China had the power to veto or block any decisions the Council tried to make.

In 1949, the Communists defeated the Nationalists on mainland China and took over all of China except for the island of Taiwan and some smaller islands off China's east coast. The Communists called their country the People's Republic of China. They claimed to be the legal government of all of China because they ruled about 98 percent of Chinese territory. They maintained that they alone and not the Nationalists should have China's seat in the UN. The United States, which was strongly anti-Communist, blocked the Communists from taking China's UN seat and kept the People's Republic of China out of the UN for more than twenty years.

In the late 1960s, the United States tried to heal the split between itself and the Communist government of China. In 1971, the United

Eleanor Roosevelt (1884-1962)

Eleanor Roosevelt was a strong supporter of the United Nations. She was the wife of President Franklin Delano Roosevelt, and when he died in April 1945, Eleanor continued to work for his dream of a United Nations.

Mrs. Roosevelt was a leader who enthusiastically supported human rights. She believed that all people are equal and should be treated with respect. In 1946, President Harry S. Truman appointed Mrs. Roosevelt as one of the first U.S. delegates to the UN. She was the only woman among the U.S. representatives.

Because she was a supporter of human rights, Mrs. Roosevelt was appointed head of the UN Commission on Human Rights, a post she held from 1946 to 1951. Mrs. Roosevelt helped write the UN's Declaration of Human Rights, one of the foundational documents of the UN. The Declaration states that "all human beings are born free and equal in dignity and right . . . without distinction of any kind such as race, color, sex, language, religion [or] political . . . opinion."

States agreed not to block the People's Republic of China from taking China's UN seat, and the Communist Chinese took their place in the United Nations and on the Security Council. Taiwan lost its membership and has been trying ever since to regain it.

In September 2002, Switzerland became the 190th member of the United Nations. Switzerland had long avoided joining the UN, feeling that its tradition of **neutrality** in world events might be destroyed if it joined the international organization. Many Swiss felt their tiny nation would have little or no voice among the major powers in the UN, and there was a strong movement in Switzerland against joining the organization. The Swiss government put the question to a vote in March 2002. The Swiss people voted 54.6 percent to 45.4 percent in favor of joining the UN.

The UN has long had offices in Geneva, Switzerland, even though the country did not belong to the UN. When the UN was formed, it took over the *Palais des Nations* (Palace of Nations), which had been built as the headquarters of the League of Nations. Today, almost nine thousand UN employees work in Geneva, and the UN bases its offices for human rights and for refugees in the city.

The *Palais des Nations* in Geneva, Switzerland, became the headquarters of the League of Nations in 1936 and is now the UN's main building outside of New York City.

Meeting Place of the World

The United Nations has locations in many parts of the world. The UN Headquarters buildings shown at the right were constructed in New York City along the East River on land donated for that purpose by the Rockefeller family.

The United Nations also has major locations in Geneva; Vienna, Austria; and Nairobi, Kenya. The UN maintains other offices in London, Rome, Paris, and dozens of other places around the world.

The General Assembly

The General Assembly is the largest organ of the United Nations and is called "the meeting place of the world." Every member nation of the United Nations has represen-

The United Nations headquarters is located on the East River of New York City. The thirty-nine-story building in the center is the Secretariat. The low white domed building on the right is the General Assembly. The low building along the river is the Conference Building.

tatives in the General Assembly, and each nation has an equal voice. A nation may have more than one representative in the General Assembly, but each nation has only one vote.

The General Assembly is the center of UN activity. Its members discuss many different issues, and most of its votes are based on simple majority rule. There are certain matters, however, that need a two-thirds majority vote to pass. Some of these special matters are the admission of

An opening session of the General Assembly is held each year in the great domed chamber.

new members to the UN, the removal of members from the UN, approval of the UN budget, and issues of international peace and security.

The General Assembly meets once a year in New York for its regular session, which usually lasts about three months. The Assembly can also be called into special sessions when needed. Six committees plus a special political committee set up by the Assembly do most of the Assembly's work throughout the year. These committees work on questions of security and **disarmament**, social and cultural matters, and the UN budget.

The General Assembly can bring matters before the Security Council and other branches of the UN. It chooses the members of the Economic and Social Council, the nonpermanent members of the Security Council, members of the Trusteeship Council, and judges on the International Court of Justice. The Assembly also appoints the UN secretary-general.

The General Assembly can make no laws. It is not a legislature like the U.S. Congress or the United Kingdom's Parliament. The General Assembly's decisions have no power over the member nations. They can choose to accept or reject the Assembly's decisions.

Money Matters

The General Assembly creates and controls the UN budget. It decides how and where the UN spends its money. The UN budget itself, however, depends on voluntary contributions from UN members. The Assembly cannot raise taxes the way Congress can. The amount of money each nation contributes is based on how rich that country is.

The United States pays the largest share of the UN budget. In the past, the United States felt that it paid too much to the UN while other countries did not pay enough. In protest against this unbalanced situation, the United States did not pay its full dues for some years. Finally, in 1999, a compromise was worked out. The UN agreed to lower the amount of money the United States pays and to raise the amounts other countries had to pay. At the end of 2002, the United States still owed half a billion dollars in back dues. The UN began 2003 in a financial crisis, having to cut staff in New York and pare back programs. Among the first nations to pay their annual dues that year were four of the countries that the UN labels LDCs, or Least Developed Countries.

Blocs and Deadlocks

In the past, the major powers of the world, such as the United States and the Soviet Union (now Russia) and their allied countries, controlled the General Assembly. A Western Bloc, or group, of countries was led by the United States, and an Eastern Bloc was led by the Soviet Union. Often deadlocks between these two opposing forces delayed or prevented UN actions on important matters. With the collapse of the Soviet Union, the Eastern Bloc no longer exists, and the UN has become more active.

Sometimes small countries unite to form small blocs to protect their interests. Today, there are strong African, Asian, and Latin American blocs in the United Nations, and these blocs often band together to balance the power of larger countries such as the United States or Russia.

The United Nations and the Creation of Israel

The area called Palestine is a strip of land on the eastern shore of the Mediterranean Sea. Palestine is the Holy Land of the Bible. The Romans conquered Palestine about the time of the birth of Jesus Christ, and in the first century A.D., they forced the Jewish inhabitants to leave the area. In the 600s, Palestine was conquered by Muslims. Eventually the region became part of the Ottoman (Turk) Empire. In 1922, following the defeat of the Ottomans in World War I, the League of Nations put Palestine under British control.

In the late 1800s, Jews began migrating to Palestine, and more went while the area was under British control. The immigrant Jewish settlers wanted to build a new Jewish homeland in Palestine. Arabs who were already living in Palestine resisted Jewish immigration, and fighting broke out. After World War II ended, Jewish groups fought the British. Eventually, the British decided to give up their control of Palestine. A plan was developed to divide Palestine into two independent countries—a Jewish state called Israel and an Arab state. The Jews in Palestine welcomed the plan, but the Arabs did not.

On November 29, 1947, the General Assembly voted 33 to 13 in favor of the plan. Ten countries did not vote. The new nation of Israel declared its independence in May 1948. The surrounding Arab states immediately attacked Israel. The UN eventually worked out a **cease-fire** between Israel and the Arabs and sent observers into the area to see that the truce was kept.

Wars between Israel and its Arab neighbors broke out in 1956, 1967, and 1973. In all three wars, UN observers were sent to the area to keep opposing troops apart. Although there has not been an all-out war since 1973, fighting has continued.

Left: Israeli troops waved good-bye in 1974 as they pulled out of territory they had occupied in the 1973 war. The cease-fire was supervised by the United Nations.

The Security Council

The Security Council of the United Nations has fifteen members, five of which are permanent. The five permanent members are China, France, Russia (the former Soviet Union), the United Kingdom, and the United States. The other ten members are nonpermanent. Every year, the

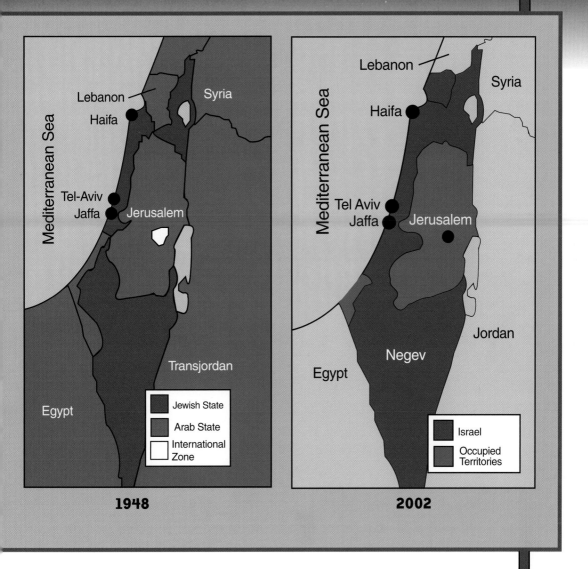

1948

2002

General Assembly appoints five member nations to the Security Council for two-year terms. The nonpermanent members are always selected so that different parts of the world have one or more seats on the Security Council.

Each member of the Council has one vote. Some matters need the votes of any nine members to pass. Other more serious matters need the votes of all the permanent members in order to pass. Any single one of the permanent members can **veto** the decision of the rest of the Council,

The Security Council is seen here voting on a matter concerning Angola in 1995. The beautiful chamber was created and donated by Norway. The vast mural shows human efforts toward peace.

thereby killing a proposed **resolution** being considered.

When the question came up of letting Communist China into the UN, the United States vetoed the idea until 1971. That year, the United States chose not to cast a vote on the issue. This allowed the question to go to the General Assembly, where no country has a veto. The Assembly voted to admit Communist China to the United Nations.

According to the UN Charter, the main job of the Security Council is to try to keep international peace and security. The Security Council considers disputes between nations or other serious threats to peace and tries to take actions to prevent them. Since 1946, the Security Council has acted numerous times in efforts to save the peace. The first major peacekeeping operation took place in Korea.

The United Nations and the Korean War

Korea is a peninsula on the eastern edge of Asia, pointing at Japan. During World War II, Korea was occupied by Japan. In the closing days of the war, the Soviet Union declared war on Japan and sent troops flooding into Korea. The United States also sent troops to Korea. The Soviets came in from the north, and the U.S. troops came in from the south.

After the war, Korea was divided into two countries, the Republic of South Korea, which was supported by the United States, and the People's Republic of North Korea, which was supported by the Soviet Union and the Communist Chinese. The United States kept troops in Korea until 1949. After the United States pulled out its forces, the North Koreans attacked South Korea on June 25, 1950.

President Harry S. Truman immediately sent U.S. troops back into Korea to help the South Koreans fight back, and the United States asked the Security Council for UN military assistance.

Under normal conditions, the Soviet Union would have vetoed any Security Council action, but at the time of the U.S. request, the Soviet Union was not attending Security Council meetings. It had left the Security Council as a protest against the fact that Nationalist China was sitting on the Security Council and not Communist China.

The Security Council acted quickly by asking the member nations of the United Nations to send military forces to aid the South Koreans. The matter then moved to

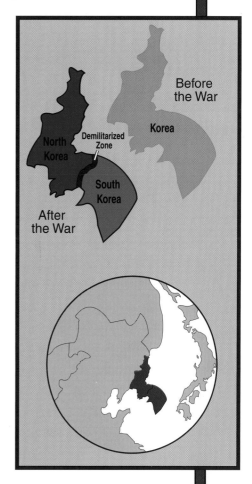

Before the War

Korea

North Korea

Demilitarized Zone

South Korea

After the War

United Nations troops aided the South Koreans in preventing a North Korean takeover in the early 1950s.

the General Assembly, where the Soviet Union could not use its veto power. The General Assembly quickly voted to have UN members use military force to stop the North Korean invasion of South Korea.

U.S. troops made up most of the UN military forces in Korea—more than half of the ground forces and almost all of the naval and air forces. The North Koreans were pushed back into their own country, but Communist China came to North Korea's aid and helped drive the UN troops back into South Korea. A **truce** ending the fighting was finally signed in 1953, but the United States still has military forces in South Korea. They watch the area between the two countries called the DMZ, for "demilitarized zone." In 2003, the United States and North Korea confronted each other diplomatically about North Korea's reviving its nuclear power program and making threats against the United States.

Other Actions

In 1960, the Security Council approved sending UN peacekeepers into the Republic of the Congo (now the Democratic Republic of the Congo) to stop the murderous civil war that had broken out there after the Republic of the Congo received its independence from Belgium. Nearly twenty thousand UN peacekeepers from twenty-nine member nations finally restored peace after four years of **intermittent** fighting.

In 1987, the Security Council sent a 350-member peacekeeping force to patrol the border between Iran and Iraq. These two countries had been at war for more than seven years. The UN forces supervised a cease-fire agreement between Iraq and Iran, but the two countries never signed a peace treaty.

Korea, the Congo, and the Iran-Iraq War are only three examples of the numerous places where the Security Council has acted to keep world peace. There have been many other occasions.

The Secretariat

In all organizations, somebody has to do the paperwork, set up meetings, and make and keep schedules. In the UN, the Secretariat does all these jobs and more. The Secretariat has its main headquarters in New York City, but it also has offices in hundreds of other places throughout the world. Over twenty thousand people work for the Secretariat, including translators who speak two or more languages, scientists, researchers, scholars, and hundreds of clerks and secretaries.

The Secretariat sets up UN negotiations to solve international conflicts and manages peacekeeping activities. It directs UN spending

Secretary-General Dag Hammarskjold went to the Congo in 1961 to help settle the civil war. He was killed when his plane crashed while flying between the two warring sides.

UN Secretaries-General

Since 1945, seven men have served as the UN secretary-general:

1945–1953: Trygve Lie of Norway
1953–1961: Dag Hammarskjøld of Sweden
1961–1971: U Thant of Burma (Myanmar)
1972–1981: Kurt Waldheim of Austria
1982–1991: Javier Pérez de Cuéllar of Peru
1992–1996: Boutros Boutros-Ghali of Egypt
1997–   : Kofi Annan of Ghana

and conducts studies on economic, social, and cultural issues. Secretariat workers must take an oath that they will work only for the UN. They must promise not to take sides in disputes and not to take directions from their home countries.

The secretary-general is the chief officer of the Secretariat and the leading figure of the United Nations. Secretaries-general are appointed by the General Assembly for five-year terms and may be reappointed.

The first secretary-general was a Norwegian, Trygve Lie, appointed on February 1, 1946. All secretaries-general except Boutros Boutros-Ghali of Egypt have been reappointed for a second term.

The secretary-general works for peace and often travels to trouble spots around the world trying to keep the peace. In 2002, Secretary-General Kofi Annan made twenty-six official visits to such places as Ukraine, Cyprus, and Mongolia.

Secretary-General U Thant met with Indian prime minister Indira Gandhi in 1967 during one of the many official visits that secretaries-general make each year.

Secretary-General Kofi Annan
and the Nobel Peace Prize

In 2001, the United Nations and Secretary-General Kofi Annan won the Nobel Peace Prize for "their work for a better organized and more peaceful world."

The UN was awarded the Peace Prize because of its efforts to achieve peace and security in the world, and Kofi Annan was honored for devoting almost his entire career to the UN. The Nobel Prize Committee said that Secretary-General Annan has brought new life to the UN.

Kofi Annan was born in Ghana in 1938, attended college in Minnesota, and began working for the United Nations in 1962. His first UN job was with the World Health Organization (WHO). He worked as a diplomat for thirty years. He was appointed secretary-general of the UN in 1997 and again in 2002. As secretary-general, Mr. Annan has led the fight against HIV/AIDS and has raised more than $1 billion in the struggle against the disease. He has also organized the UN battle against international terrorism.

Chapter Three

Taking on Other Tasks

The General Assembly, Security Council, and Secretariat are only three of the major branches, or organs, of the United Nations. On an equal footing with them are the Economic and Social Council, the Trusteeship Council, and the International Court of Justice (ICJ). As the organization chart on the facing page shows, only the Trusteeship Council and the ICJ do not have large numbers of other commissions, committees, and programs under them.

The Economic and Social Council

The Economic and Social Council (ECOSOC) helps people live better lives through its efforts in fighting hunger and disease and by training them for jobs so they can become economically self-sufficient. ECOSOC has fifty-four members from many different parts of the world. The General Assembly appoints eighteen members to ECOSOC every year for three-year terms.

Some of the organizations shown in the chart under ECOSOC are not actually part of the UN but work with it. These organizations are called Specialized Agencies.

The World Health Organization (WHO) is one of the better-known Specialized Agencies. WHO was founded on April 7, 1948, to try to

In New Delhi, India, a woman and her child read WHO posters about the distribution of polio vaccine.

The United Nations System

Principal Organs of the United Nations

International Court of Justice	Security Council	General Assembly	Economic & Social Council	Trusteeship Council	Secretariat

Programs and Funds
- UN Conference on Trade and Development
- UN Drug Control Program
- UN Environment Program
- UN Human Settlements Program (UN-Habitat)
- UN Development Program
- UNIFEM-UN Development Fund for Women
- UNV-UN Volunteers
- UNFPA-UN Population Fund
- UNHCR-Office of the UN High Commissioner for Refugees
- UNICEF-UN Children's Fund
- WFP-World Food Program
- UNRWA-UN Relief and Works Agency for Palestine Refugees in the Near East

International Atomic Energy Agency

World Trade Organization

World Tourism Organization

PrepCom for the Nuclear-Test-Ban-Treaty Organization

Organization for the Prohibition of Chemical Weapons

Specialized Agencies
- International Labor Organization
- Food & Agriculture Organizations of the UN
- UN Educational, Scientific, and Cultural Organization
- World Health Organization
- World Bank Group
  - IBRD-International Bank for Reconstruction and Development
  - IDA-International Development Association
  - IFC-International Finance Corporation
  - MIGA- Miltilateral Investment Guarantee Agency
  - International Centre for Settlement of Investment Disputes
- International Monetary Fund
- International Civil Aviation Organization
- International Maritime Organization
- International Telecommunication Union
- Universal Postal Union
- World Meteorological Organization
- World Intellectual Property Organization
- International Fund for Agricultural Development
- UN Industrial Development Organization

- UN Office at Geneva
- UN Office at Vienna
- UN Office at Nairobi

27

Literacy as Freedom

In 2003, the United Nations began the "Literacy Decade—Education for All" campaign. Led by UNESCO, the campaign recognizes that almost one billion people cannot take part in the swift changes occurring in modern technological societies. More than one hundred million children have no access to school at all, and many others drop out before they are fully able to read. During the Literacy Decade, which will last through 2012, each UN agency will do the work it can do best on local, national, and international levels to promote literacy.

build "universal peace through health for all." April 7th is known as World Health Day. WHO is dedicated to wiping out the world's deadliest diseases, such as AIDS, tuberculosis (TB), malaria, polio, tetanus, and diphtheria. These diseases kill millions of people every year. WHO also works to provide better health care for mothers and for pregnant women. WHO workers can be found in many parts of the world educating people about safe drinking water, better eating habits, and general health care.

Another well-known Specialized Agency is UNESCO—the United Nations Educational, Scientific and Cultural Organization. The goal of UNESCO is to help wipe out the causes of war by fighting disease, poverty, and ignorance. Among other activities, UNESCO helps educate millions of people throughout the world. UNESCO also trains teachers and pays for building new schools.

One program carried out by UNESCO is World Heritage, which encourages the recognition and preservation of places that are important in human history. The Acropolis in Athens, Greece, is one such site.

The Trusteeship Council

Many countries that fought in World War I had colonies throughout the world. The countries that were defeated in the war lost their colonies. The

League of Nations gave supervision of these colonies to some of the nations that won the war. The colonies were renamed trust territories.

Many of these trust territories became independent countries by the end of World War II. The United Kingdom, the United States, France, Italy, Belgium, Australia, the Netherlands, New Zealand, and South Africa all had some trust territories when the war ended in 1945.

The UN Charter set up a Trusteeship Council to supervise how these lands were governed by the countries that controlled them. South Africa was the only country that refused to let its trust territory come under UN supervision. South West Africa remained under the old League of Nations rules until it became independent as Namibia in 1990.

In 1956, a UN visiting mission went to New Guinea, which was at that time an Australian trust territory. The eastern half became independent as Papua New Guinea in 1975.

Most of the trust territories in 1945 were in Africa under British, French, or Belgian control. The trust territories under U.S. control were all located in the Western Pacific. All the nations that had trust territories were members of the Trusteeship Council. China and the Soviet Union did not have trust territories, but they also sat on the Council, as did a group of members elected by the General Assembly.

The chief obligation of the Trusteeship Council was to "promote the political, social, and educational advancement" of the peoples living in the trust territories. The council worked to improve living conditions and to promote the independence of the trusteeship lands through education and economic development.

Palau

Indonesia

Palau – the Last Trust Territory

The big guns on the American battleships roared to life on the morning of September 15, 1944, and thousands of shells slammed into the hills and beaches of Peleliu, a small island in the western Pacific Ocean. Peleliu was and is part of the Palau group of three hundred islands. It was a Japanese stronghold in World War II.

When U.S. Marines invaded Peleliu that September morning, one of the bloodiest battles of World War II began. The Japanese had dug hundreds of caves on the island, and they fought hard to keep their positions. Ever so slowly, the Marines took the island foot by bloody foot. The battle ended in victory for the Marines on November 25, but the last Japanese soldiers went into hiding and did not surrender until February 1945.

The Palau islands had been under German control before World War I. The Japanese forced the Germans out of the islands during the war, and the League of Nations put the Palau islands under Japanese protection after the war ended. The Japanese turned Peleliu into a military fortress, and no foreigners were allowed to visit the islands after 1935.

The islands came under the protection of the United States after World War II. They were part of the Trust Territory of the Pacific Islands set up by the United Nations. The United States gave up its trusteeship in 1986, and the Republic of Palau officially came into being on October 1, 1994, after it chose independence over joining the Federated States of Micronesia. The photo above shows one of the young Palau men who depend on fishing for a living.

Eventually, all of the trusteeship lands became independent nations. The last trusteeship was Palau, a group of islands in the Western Pacific under U.S. trusteeship. Palau became independent in 1994. Because all the trusteeship lands once under the supervision of the Trusteeship Council had become independent nations, the Trusteeship Council's operations were suspended in 1994.

The International Court of Justice

Attempts to create a world court to settle legal disputes between nations go back to the late 1800s. In 1920, an international court was established as part of the League of Nations. When the United Nations was created, this court became the International Court of Justice. Although it is one of the six major organs of the UN, the court is actually semi-independent.

The Court meets at the Hague in the Netherlands. The fifteen judges on the Court are appointed by the Security Council and the General Assembly. The judges are appointed for nine-year terms—five judges every three years. Nine of the fifteen judges must be present to hear a case, and decisions are made by majority vote. Decisions are final and cannot be appealed.

The Court can hear all cases involving international law, but only if both countries involved in a dispute agree to let the Court hear their case. No country can be forced to go to the Court, and no country has to follow a Court decision. However, countries have found it easier and less expensive to let the Court decide a case than to drag a dispute on for years with no agreement ever being reached.

In 1983, the African countries of Burkina Faso and Mali could not agree on the location of their common international border. They took their case to the International Court of Justice, which settled the dispute in 1986.

The International Court of Justice in the Hague delivered a decision in 2002.

The Trial of Slobodan Milosevic

The International Court of Justice is not the only United Nations court. The UN can set up other courts when it sees fit to do so. In May 1993, the Security Council formed the International Criminal **Tribunal** for the former Yugoslavia (ICTY). The Tribunal was created to look into the crimes committed during the civil war in the former nation of Yugoslavia.

The ICTY is located in the Hague, the Netherlands. It has sixteen permanent judges appointed by the General Assembly for four-year terms. The goal of the ICTY is to bring to trial those people in the former country of Yugoslavia accused of committing crimes against humanity, such as the slaughter of innocent civilians.

The president of Yugoslavia during its civil war was Slobodan Milosevic. The ICTY charged him with **war crimes,** accusing him of thirty-two counts of war crimes, sixty-six counts of crimes against humanity, and **genocide** in the deaths of nine hundred ethnic Albanians in the former Yugoslav state of Kosovo. In the photo above, French investigators carefully explored a mass grave found in 1999.

The trial of Milosevic was the first time a person had been tried for war crimes since the end of World War II. At that time, leaders of the Nazi Party in Germany and some Japanese leaders were tried for war crimes. Those found guilty were either executed or sent to prison.

Milosevic was taken to the Hague for his trial. He pleaded not guilty of all accusations and defended himself by claiming that the Tribunal did not have the right to try him.

The Peacekeepers

The main purpose of the United Nations is to try to keep peace in the world. Sometimes this means sending UN observers into an area where trouble has developed between two countries to keep warring sides apart. On occasion, peacekeeping means actually fighting against **aggressors**.

UN peacekeeping missions depend on the willingness of UN member nations to supply the forces needed to accomplish the mission. Peacekeeping forces are usually made up of troops from a number of member nations. The peacekeepers are part of a member nation's military forces. Individual countries volunteer their troops to be part of UN peacekeeping forces. Peacekeepers usually come from smaller neutral countries not involved in the dispute in the country to which they are sent. Private individuals cannot volunteer to join a peacekeeping force. All UN peacekeeping missions are under the control of the UN Security Council.

Early Missions

One of the first UN observer teams—UN forces were not called peacekeepers at that time—was sent into Greece in 1947. Democratic and Communist Greeks were fighting a civil war for control of the country, and Greece's Communist neighbors to the north were sending men and supplies into Greece to help

UN peacekeepers in Honduras destroyed captured weapons used by rebels in the civil war in 1990.

the Greek Communists. The UN observers were sent to make certain Greece's northern neighbors did not cross into Greece. Eventually, the Communists were defeated, and Greece remained an independent democratic country.

UN observers were also sent into Indonesia in 1947. Indonesia had once been a colony of the Netherlands. The Indonesians wanted independence, and the Dutch resisted. The UN played a major role in creating the independent Republic of Indonesia in 1949.

The Suez Canal Crisis

The United Nations has been involved in Arab-Israeli conflicts since the late 1940s. In 1956, UN peacekeepers were called upon to keep Israeli and Egyptian forces apart during a war over the use of the Suez Canal.

Yugoslav soldiers served as peacekeepers in Egypt during the Suez Canal crisis. In January 1957, they patrolled El Arish, Egypt.

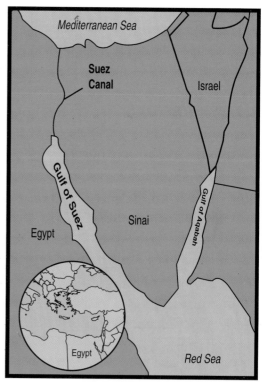

The Suez Canal, built by the French in the nineteenth century, connects the Red Sea and the Mediterranean Sea. The canal is in the Sinai Desert on Egyptian territory, but it was under control of the British and the French until 1956, when Egypt took control of the canal and closed it to Israeli shipping.

Israeli troops attacked the canal, and the British and French sent in troops to help the Israelis. The UN General Assembly called for a cease-fire and sent a peacekeeping force into the Sinai to separate the two sides. The UN peacekeepers set up camp on the Egyptian side of the Israel-Egypt border. The Israelis would not allow UN forces on their side of the border. The UN force continued to patrol the border until 1967, when the Egyptians finally asked the UN Peacekeepers to leave.

The Iran-Iraq War of 1980-88

Iraq invaded Iran in 1980, beginning a long war between the two countries. Secretary-General Kurt Waldheim called on both countries to stop fighting, but they ignored him. The Security Council passed a resolution calling for a cease-fire and troop withdrawals, but the fighting continued.

Iraq and Iran both claimed that chemical weapons were being used and that civilians were being killed. UN investigators reported that Iraq was indeed using chemical weapons. The Security Council condemned the use of chemical weapons as a violation of international treaties.

In 1987, the Security Council again called for an end to the war. This time, both sides accepted the Security Council's recommendations. In 1988, the UN sent a peacekeeping force to observe the cease-fire. Iran and Iraq never signed a peace treaty, but the UN was successful in bringing an end to the fighting.

The Persian Gulf War

Sometimes UN forces are needed to stop an aggressor nation. In 1950, UN forces were sent to Korea to stop the North Korean invasion of South

Korea. On August 2, 1990, Iraqi forces stormed across the Kuwait border and overran the small country in less than two days. The United Nations Security Council condemned the attack and called for Iraq to pull back its forces. Iraq refused to do so.

Led by the United States in a military campaign called Desert Storm, an international UN force attacked Iraq in February 1991. Iraq was defeated in only a few days, and it pulled back its forces from Kuwait. The UN then passed a series of resolutions calling for inspection teams to enter Iraq to search for weapons. The Iraqis allowed the UN teams into the country at first, but they later forced the UN teams to leave. UN inspectors were not allowed back into the country until late 2002, when the United States and Iraq were about to go to war. The United States and the United Kingdom invaded Iraq in 2003 without waiting for a discovery by the inspection teams who were searching for nuclear, biological, and chemical weapons of mass destruction.

Bosnia-Herzegovina

Genocide is an effort to wipe out an entire group of people. During World War II, Germany was guilty of genocide against Jews, Rom (often called Gypsies), and other groups of people. About six million Jews were killed during the war. In the 1990s, the monstrosity of genocide occurred again in Yugoslavia.

Yugoslavia was a united country between 1918 and 1991. It was made up of a number of smaller states, just as the United States is made up of fifty smaller states. The largest of Yugoslavia's states, or republics, were Serbia, Bosnia-Herzegovina, and Croatia. The people in these republics were divided by different traditions and religions. Most Bosnians were Muslims. Most Serbs belonged to the Eastern Orthodox Church. Most Croats were Roman Catholics.

In 1991, the former Yugoslavia began to break up into separate independent countries. The more powerful Serbs tried to stop the

Muslim residents of Stari Vitez in Bosnia-Herzegovina stood in front of their partially destroyed home in 1994.

Bosnians from breaking away and forming their own country. They attacked Bosnia and killed as many Bosnian Muslims as they could. Serbs rounded up groups of Muslim Bosnians and put them into prison camps. Many innocent civilians were killed, and entire towns were wiped out. The term "**ethnic cleansing**" was used to describe their treatment.

In 1992, United Nation peacekeepers were sent to Bosnia. The UN peacekeepers were volunteers from some of the member nations of the UN. The UN forces were known as the Blue Helmets because of the blue helmets they wore. At first, the peacekeepers were allowed only to provide food, clothing, and medicine to the suffering people. The peacekeepers were not supposed to use force, but soon they came under attack and had to use force to defend themselves.

When terrorists crashed hijacked airplanes into the Twin Towers of New York's World Trade Center on September 11, 2001, killing almost three thousand people, a whole new type of warfare was started.

UN involvement in the war helped bring about an end to the horror in Bosnia. In 1995, President Bill Clinton got the leaders of the three warring states—Serbia, Bosnia, and Croatia—together to sign a peace treaty. For several years, the genocide stopped. In 1998, it began again in the former Yugoslavia state of Kosovo.

Once again, the Serbs were accused of ethnic cleansing, this time against Kosovo's Albanians. In March 1999, air forces from the North Atlantic Treaty Organization (NATO) began a bombing campaign against the Serbs. The fighting ended, and the president of the former Yugoslavia, Slobodan Milosevic, was later put on trial for war crimes. In 2003, a new nation, Serbia & Montenegro, formed from Yugoslavia, and the name Yugoslavia was dropped. The two former republics have an option to separate into two countries in several years.

The War on Terrorism

On September 11, 2001, terrorists hijacked two airliners and crashed them into the Twin Towers of the World Trade Center in New York City. At the same time, more terrorists crashed another plane into the

Pentagon in Washington, D.C. A fourth plane was also hijacked, but the passengers bravely fought the hijackers and forced the aircraft to crash into a field in Pennsylvania before it could damage structures and take more lives. On that day, a new type of war began.

The United States declared a "War on Terrorism" and asked for UN help with it. The United Nations Security Council responded by setting up a Counterterrorism Committee and called on "Member States to prevent and suppress the financing of terrorism, refrain from providing any support to entities or persons involved in terrorist acts, and deny safe haven to those who finance, plan, support and commit such acts."

The United States led an invasion into Afghanistan in 2002 seeking to destroy the terrorist network al-Qaeda, which was supported by the Afghanistan government. That government, run by a religious group called the Taliban, was overthrown, and a new government was set up. The al-Qaeda network of terrorists suffered greatly but was not destroyed, and Osama bin Laden, its leader, was not captured.

The War on Terrorism will probably continue into the foreseeable future. It is unlike any other war ever fought because there is no single enemy and no one battlefield. By spring 2003, terrorist attacks had been carried out in such places as Bali, Kenya, Yemen, Morocco, and Saudi Arabia. Clearly, the war on terrorism is universal.

Disarmament

World War II ended only after the United States dropped two atomic bombs on Japan. At first, only the United States had "the Bomb," but in 1949, the Soviet Union tested its own atomic bomb.

A Nobel for the Peacekeepers

In 1988, the UN Peacekeeping Forces were awarded the Nobel Peace Prize. The Nobel Committee recognized the organization for "reducing tensions where an armistice has been negotiated but a peace treaty has yet to be established. In situations of this kind, the UN forces represent the manifest will of the community of nations to achieve peace through negotiations, and the forces have, by their presence, made a decisive contribution towards the initiation of actual peace negotiations."

The United States used two atomic bombs on Japan in 1945 to bring about an end to World War II. The UN established a Disarmament Commission to be sure that atomic weapons are not used again.

Even worse weapons were soon being developed. In 1952, the United States exploded the world's first hydrogen bomb, a weapon so powerful that it required an atomic bomb to set it off. The atomic and hydrogen bombs are called nuclear or thermonuclear weapons because they use the awesome energy in the nucleus of atoms as a weapon.

Since the 1950s, other countries have developed nuclear weapons. Among them are the United Kingdom, France, China, India, and others. One of the major goals of the United Nations is to stop the further spread of all kinds of weapons—weapons used for chemical warfare, biological warfare, and especially nuclear warfare. The UN is also trying to get countries to get rid of their weapons, or disarm.

Disarmament is not a new idea. The League of Nations tried to get its member nations to reduce the number of weapons they had after World War I. At first the League was successful, but in the 1930s, all the major nations of the world began to rearm themselves. This rearming helped lead to World War II. After that war, the new United Nations tried to get its member nations to limit the weapons they had, but such limitation has not been successful.

In 1952, the United Nations set up a Disarmament Commission, which worked with the major nuclear powers to reduce nuclear testing. In 1963, the United States, the United Kingdom, and the Soviet Union signed a treaty banning the testing of nuclear weapons in the atmosphere, in outer space, and on the ocean floor.

UN Peacekeeping Today

Until the end of the Cold War in about 1990, the United Nations had sent UN observer teams into more than a dozen trouble spots throughout the world, from Guatemala in Central America to the Congo in Africa to Pakistan in Asia. Since the end of the Cold War, UN peacekeeping missions have increased dramatically. In the 1990s, the number of UN peacekeepers in the world increased to about ninety-three thousand.

UN peacekeepers are often involved in situations where one country is opposing another or where one faction in a nation is in a civil war with another. The peacekeeping troops come into the situation as neutral figures willing to be helpful.

UN forces have been used in many ways. The UN Blue Helmets supervise elections, give out food, and help refugees find new places to live. The peacekeepers also operate mine-clearing activities, trying to find and destroy the millions of land mines buried under former battlefields of the world.

There is not nearly enough money or equipment to carry out all the activities the Blue Helmets are asked to do. Yet the UN is frequently asked for their help. The UN has set up a new office called the Department of Peacekeeping Operations to supervise all the many activities of UN peacekeepers.

In 2000, one of the tasks of the UN peacekeepers in East Timor was to build benches for a school that had been destroyed in a civil war.

Chapter Five

Agents of Assistance

The United Nations often becomes the focus of controversy. No member nation has always agreed with everything the Security Council has decided to do. Not even the whole Security Council has always agreed. Many votes have been taken on subjects that have been vetoed by one or another of the permanent members of the Security Council.

There is often less argument about the things the UN does to help bring about development and change in the lives of the people of the member nations. In addition to those Specialized Agencies already discussed, other Specialized Agencies work to remove the underlying causes of war. The Food and Agricultural Organization (FAO), for example, works to wipe out hunger.

The World Bank provides money needed by poor countries to build farms, industries, and other sources of economic wealth. The International Labor Organization helps improve working conditions for workers and is trying to wipe out child labor. The International Atomic Energy Agency promotes the safe and peaceful use of nuclear energy.

United Nations organizations work to achieve equality for women, more opportunities for the disabled, and the resettlement of refugees.

The UN's Food and Agricultural Organization is charged with helping to wipe out hunger around the world. Representatives of the FAO worked in Sénégal, Africa, in 1974 to help the local Senegalese fishermen make better use of ocean resources to feed their people.

Cambodian children played near a memorial featuring the skulls of some of the thousands of people killed during the terrible Communist Khmer Rouge regime in the 1970s. UNICEF tries to protect children in both war and peace.

Concern for Children—UNICEF

One of the best-known Specialized Agencies of the UN is the United Nations Children's Fund, or UNICEF, which is designed to help children. This organization was set up during the very first meeting of the UN in 1946. World War II had uprooted millions of children in Europe and Asia, and these children desperately needed shelter, food, and health care. The UN set up the United Nations International Children's Emergency Fund to aid these victims of the long war.

UNICEF focused on helping the children of World War II return to normal lives. After the crisis was over, the UN decided to help the children living in the poorer nations of the world—the so-called developing nations. The new organization to help children was called the United Nations Children's Fund, but the UN kept the acronym UNICEF.

UNICEF trains teachers to work with children. It supplies equipment and materials to build schools, and it runs health clinics for children. The organization teaches mothers and children how to eat properly and how to avoid disease by practicing good health habits.

Many young people in the United States and Canada have donated or raised money for UNICEF in special fund drives. UNICEF also sells greeting cards throughout the world to help raise money.

UNICEF workers travel to many different and sometimes dangerous places. They often can be found working in countries where civil wars are still raging. Many UNICEF workers dedicate their lives to helping children survive and prosper. In 1965, UNICEF was awarded the Nobel Peace Prize.

The flags of all the member nations fly on the Plaza at the United Nations building in New York City.

The UN also assists people affected by natural disasters such as floods, hurricanes, and earthquakes. Over the years, the UN has set up groups to fight crime and international drug trafficking.

The UN Today

The United Nations is not the same organization now that it was in 1945. It has grown from fifty original members to 191. In 1945, many of the lands in Africa and Southeast Asia were colonies belonging to the world's most powerful nations. Today these former colonies have become independent countries and are member nations of the UN.

The majority of nations in the UN are located in the developing parts of the world—Latin America, Africa, the Middle East, and Asia. The goals of these countries are often different from the goals of the more powerful nations of the world such as the United States, Russia, the United Kingdom, and Germany. Many of these developing nations joined France, Germany, China, and Russia in opposing the United States and the United Kingdom when it planned to invade Iraq in 2003.

Over the years, the United Nations has had many successes and many failures, but on the whole, the world seems to be a better place with the UN than it would have been without it. There have been many small, localized wars since 1945, but the UN has played a major role in providing a forum for the peaceful resolution of differences.

Time Line

1914 World War I begins.

1918 World War I ends, and many people recognize the need for an organization to help prevent wars.

1920 League of Nations is formed; the United States does not join.

1939 World War II begins, ending the League of Nations, which was officially dissolved in 1946.

1945 World War II ends; people are again determined to form an organization to help prevent future wars.

1945 United Nations Charter is signed; the United States joins.

1946 General Assembly and Security Council meet for first time; Trygve Lie is appointed first UN secretary-general.

1948 The UN is instrumental in establishing the Jewish nation of Israel in Palestine; the first Arab-Israeli War begins.

1950 Korean War begins.

1953 Korean War truce is signed.

1956 Arab-Israeli War again breaks out; UN peacekeepers are sent in.

1965 Nobel Peace Prize awarded to UNICEF.

1967 Once more, Arab-Israeli War breaks out.

1973 Third Arab-Israeli War breaks out; UN sends a peacekeeping force to the Middle East again.

1980 Iran-Iraq War begins.

1988 UN brings end to fighting between Iran and Iraq.

1990 Iraq invades Kuwait, setting off the Persian Gulf War.

2001 World Trade Center Towers in New York City and part of the Pentagon in Washington, D.C., are destroyed. The War on Terrorism begins.

2001 Nobel Peace Prize is awarded to Secretary-General Kofi Annan and the United Nations.

2002 UN sends arms inspection teams to Iraq.

2003 American and British troops invade Iraq without approval of the Security Council.

Glossary

aggressor a person, group, or nation that attacks

cease-fire an agreement to halt fighting

charter written statement of principles and organization; a constitution

Cold War political conflict between 1948 and 1990 with Western
democracies on one side and Communist nations on the other side

disarmament reduction or destruction of weapons of war owned by
a country

ethnic cleansing expulsion, imprisonment, and killing of an ethnic
minority by a dominant majority group

genocide destruction of an entire group of people because of their race,
color, or religion

human rights rights that people are entitled to just by being born. The
right not to be murdered is a basic human right.

intermittent not continuous

neutrality a situation of being independent, not taking one side or the
other in a conflict

puppet government a government established by an outside force, giving
the appearance of a legitimate government but actually controlled by
the outsiders

refugee a person who flees his or her home area or country because of
war, hunger, or other serious threat

resolution a formal expression of the will of a group

tribunal a court

truce cease-fire

veto to block a resolution from passing

war crime a crime such as genocide that is committed on a massive scale
under cover of war

To Find Out More

BOOKS

Jacobs, William Jay. *Search for Peace: The Story of the United Nations.* Scribner, 1994.

Melvern, Linda. *United Nations.* World Organizations Series. Watts, 2000.

Patterson, Charles. *Oxford 50th Anniversary Book of the United Nations.* Oxford University Press, 1995.

ADDRESSES AND WEB SITES

United Nations
Department of Public Information
New York, NY 10017
www.un.org

CyberSchoolBus: United Nations Global Teaching and Learning Project
www.un.org/Pubs/CyberSchoolBus/

UNICEF
www.unicef.org/

UNESCO
www.unesco.org/

Index